GW00724737

THE PERFECT SETTING

First published 2000 by Black & White Publishing Ltd, Edinburgh

ISBN 1 902927 18 4

Text © Graham Lironi 2000

Recipes © Costley & Costley Ltd 2000

Photographs © Paul Dodds 2000

British Library Catalogue in Publishing Data: A Catalogue record for this book is available

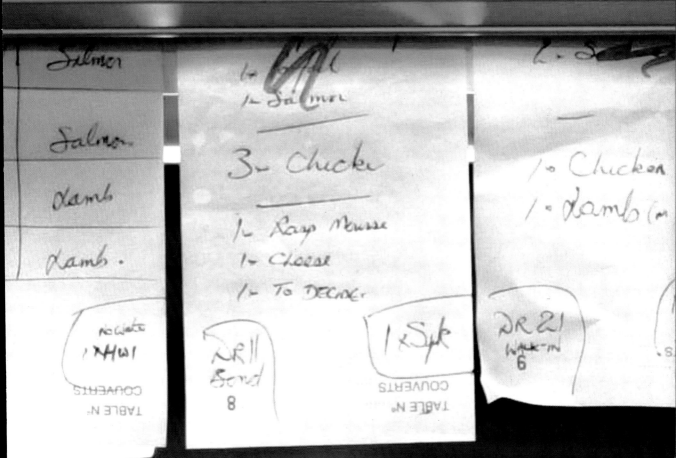

THE PERFECT SETTING

THE COSTLEY & COSTLEY STORY

TEXT BY GRAHAM LIRONI

PHOTOGRAPHS BY PAUL DODDS

Acknowledgments

We wish to extend our appreciation and gratitude to our loyal, hard-working Directors and staff for their continued efforts in maintaining the high quality and standards expected of them and without whom there wouldn't be the growth in our business.

We are indebted to our customers, especially those who return again and again and for whom we strive to attain the highest standards possible. We acknowledge our suppliers who always deliver on time and have never let us down in an emergency.

Finally, without the support and encouragement of our family and friends none of this would have been possible. Heartfelt thanks to all.

Cath & Bill Costley

CHAPTER ONE

THE CHEF

THE CHEF

Costley & Costley Hoteliers' motto, as depicted on the entrance gates to Lochgreen Country House Hotel, reads 'Ad Virtutem Nitens', which translates as 'the pursuit of excellence'. It is this pursuit which underlies the Ayrshire company's daily endeavour to exceed the expectations of each of its guests and underpins the remarkable story of the transition of its proprietor from an underprivileged trainee chef to a successful entrepreneur.

Bill Costley was born on 1st May 1952 in Dumfries. A middle child, with an older and younger sister, his family hailed from Whithorn in Wigtownshire. His father ran a greengrocer and his mother was a farm worker. At the age of four, the family moved to Prestwick, where Bill attended primary school before progressing to Prestwick Academy.

As a schoolboy Bill was interested in art, for which he had a natural aptitude, and sport (particularly football). Both interests have had a lasting influence throughout his life. It was also at school, in a presentiment of his future choice of career, that he could be found selling his own home-made cakes and tablet to fellow pupils. A born entrepreneur!

His father left the family home when Bill was ten
years old. Naturally this was a very traumatic time
for the family and had a significant influence on him.
After leaving school at the age of fifteen without
qualifications – one of the biggest regrets in Bill's
life – his mother managed to secure him a job at
Gardiners the Bakers in Prestwick, where she herself
worked. This was to be Bill's initiation into the catering
trade. He also worked at Smiley's The Fish Shop in
Prestwick as a delivery boy, before quickly progressing
to become a poulterer and fishmonger, an experience
which was to be of great benefit to him in later life.
At his mother's suggestion, Bill enrolled at Ayr College
where, on completion of a two-year course giving him
a practical introduction to cooking, he attained his
147 and 151 City & Guilds Certificates. The course
proved to be a revelation: for the first time in his life
Bill found something he was really good at, and he
discovered, much to his surprise, that he enjoyed
studying. He decided that he wanted to become
a chef. On completion of his course, he took a job
in the kitchen at the South Beach Hotel in Troon.

However, heeding his mother's wise advice that he should seek the security of employment that can only be gained from a bigger and better establishment, at the age of seventeen he applied for, and was accepted to, a live-in position at the renowned Turnberry Hotel. This was at a time when British Transport Hotels was regarded as *the* training organisation in the catering trade and most successful chefs in Scotland learned their skills through that route. Leaving home proved to be something of a culture shock though. He worked six days a week, from nine o'clock in the morning till midnight. He describes it now as a strict, army-type regime and recalls that, on the Monday morning he started, he was one of six commis chefs, but by the Friday, he was one of only two remaining. Dedication might well have been necessary for survival but, although the regime was undoubtedly very strict, it stood young Bill and many others in good stead. Regrettably, that situation has changed in recent years, and British Transport Hotels has been sold off to the private sector, with the loss of a superb training ground for young chefs.

When he finished his training, Bill left Turnberry
with the intention of travelling to The Park Hotel
at Interlaken in Switzerland, a country which, along
with France, is regarded within the catering trade as
one of the best training grounds in the world for chefs.
However, two months prior to receiving a work permit,
Bill landed a job at the newly built, 120 bedroom
Caledonian Hotel in Ayr, where he met his future
wife Catherine, already employed there as a cashier.
His plans for moving to Switzerland were indefinitely
postponed. Bill started work at The Caledonian as a
commis chef and, two years later, became the head
chef with responsibility over a brigade of eighteen.
On reflection, he considers that he was perhaps
too young for such a weight of responsibility, but
acknowledges that he was ambitious and that, in
addition to honing his culinary expertise, the position
taught him a vast amount about man management,
effective delegation and leadership; all vital business
tools put to good use as his career progressed.

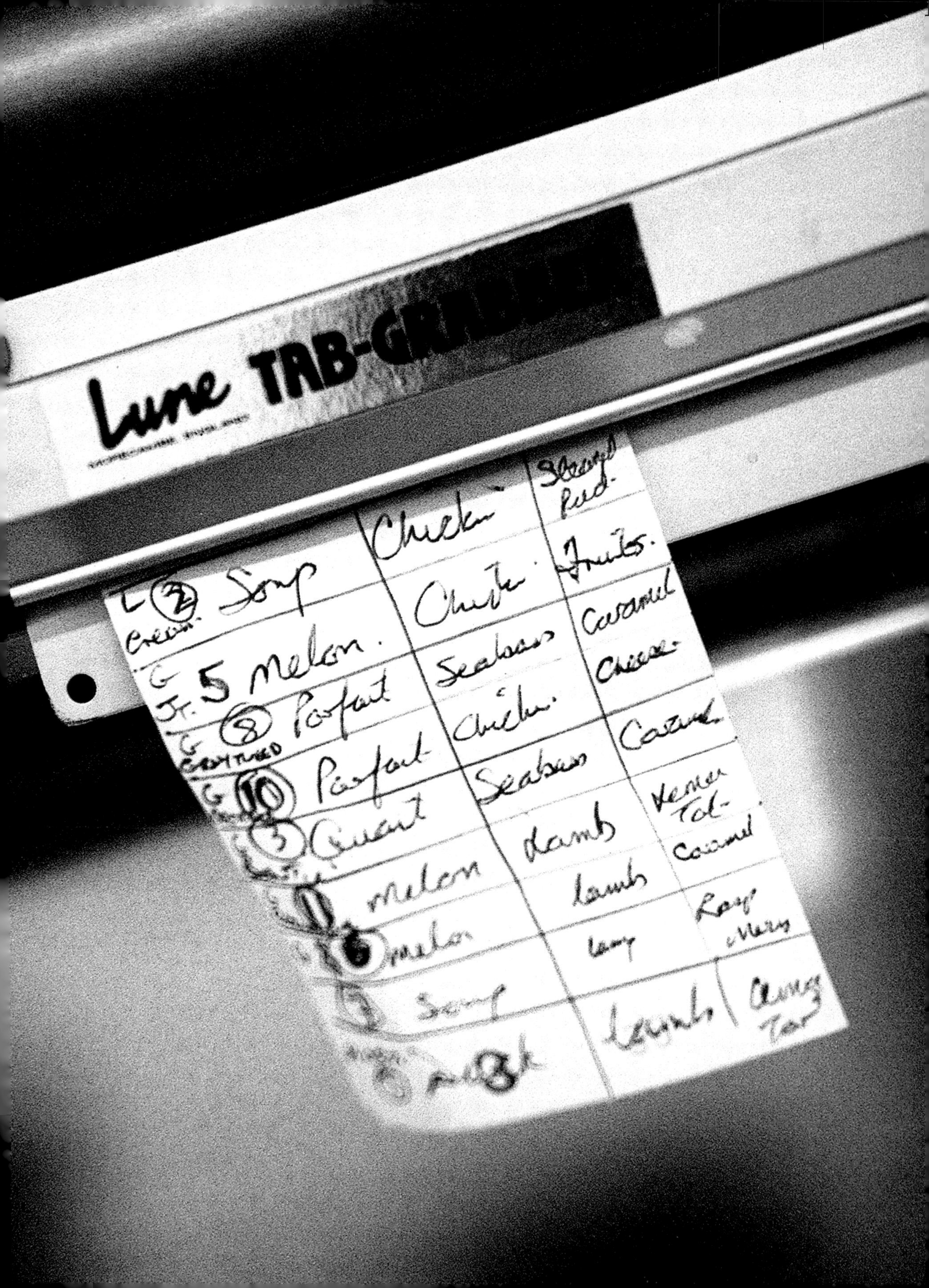
Lune
Soup
5 melon.
Seabass
Caramel
Cheese
Parfait
Lamb
Caramel
lamb

In the early to mid 1970s, the catering trade in
Britain underwent a number of significant changes.
There were, for example, huge advances in the range
of equipment and machinery used in kitchens, and
this, combined with the introduction of nouvelle
cuisine, was revolutionising the industry. Suddenly
catering had become big business in the UK. More
and more people began eating out more often and,
when they did, they were becoming more adventurous
with food; more willing to experiment with unfamiliar
dishes and flavours. These changes meant that, for the
first time, a new generation of chefs was able to shed
the constricting straitjacket of traditional recipes and
use their new-found freedom to express individual
culinary talents with flair and imagination. This
new-found freedom suited Bill's artistic temperament
perfectly. He remained at The Caledonian for most
of the following decade, a period during which he was
able to build himself a formidable local reputation as
a gifted chef by entering and winning a range of culinary
competitions. By this time Bill's chief ambition was
to have his own business. He considered competitions

as a means of furthering his career and helping him realise this ambition. However, Bill's entrance into competitive cooking got off to an inauspicious start when he applied for a competition organised through Ayr College, where he had returned to attend an advanced cookery course on a part-time basis shortly after his marriage, earning himself a 7063 City & Guilds Certificate. When Bill failed to win any prizes, he was furious with himself for not dedicating himself sufficiently to the competition. But determination is one of the Costley trademarks, and he soon won his first competition, followed by many others. His subsequent success in competitions covered a considerable array of culinary skills, including decorative, marzipan, carving and buffet work. Success meant that he began to garner recognition which, in turn, helped fill the restaurant. When he won Gold in a national competition run from London, his fame spread and he found himself in demand by a string of renowned hotels in London for freelance decorative work, enabling him to capitalise on his by now well-developed artistic flair.

CHAPTER TWO

HIGHGROVE HOUSE HOTEL

Situated high on a hill, with panoramic views over the Ayrshire coastline, from the Firth of Clyde to the Isle of Arran and beyond to the Mull of Kintyre, Highgrove House Hotel was originally built by a sea captain in the 1920s.

It opened under its present name in 1988 as a traditional nine-bedroom hotel. The next few years were spent reinvesting operating profits in an extensive renovation and refurbishment programme for the property, including building a new kitchen and extension.

Bill is keen to pay tribute to the huge contribution made to the success of the business by his wife Catherine. The couple worked from six o'clock in the morning until midnight every day for six years without a day off work, despite the fact that when they bought Highgrove, their elder son (Bill) was about to leave school (he is now a doctor) and their younger son (Andrew) was still at primary school (he is now a chef at Lochgreen House). Bill is quick to stress the importance of the active role played by his sons' grandparents, Bill and Ella Hutchison, who helped look after them whilst Bill and his wife were unable to escape the demands of the fledgling business. He is convinced that the business would not have been so successful without their help. Another important ally was the bank manager at that time, a family friend named David Hodgson who played an important role in the early years of the business through his assistance and advice in the installation of valuable management accounting systems and procedures.

At Highgrove, Cath worked as the front of house manageress while Bill managed the kitchens. Both are hard workers who stress the importance of attention to detail when it comes to standards of service. It is this comprehensive application of high housekeeping standards that is the distinctive feature of Costley and Costley's establishments.

It was soon after setting up Highgrove House that Bill was approached to join the Scottish Culinary Team, whose other members were Peter Jackson, William Gibb, Ferrier Richardson and Charles Price. When he proceeded to win a gold medal at an international competition in Frankfurt – the first gold medal that

a Scottish chef had ever won in Germany – he found himself on the front page of *The Glasgow Herald*. Such publicity did Highgrove House no harm whatsoever. Bill remained an integral member of the team for the next six years and played an active role in the winning of a silver medal in Singapore. However, he eventually had to bring his involvement to a conclusion when he realised that the time commitment it required began to conflict with the more pressing demands of building his own business.

Whilst the welcome publicity generated by winning international culinary competitions might have attracted customers to investigate the offering at Highgrove, Bill showed considerable foresight in his realisation from the outset that such public recognition was no foundation on which to build a sustainable business. Whilst a high public profile might well have an initially beneficial impact on a restaurant, it would never attract repeat custom to Highgrove unless the restaurant was able to deliver a standard of service that matched its clientèle's high expectations; and if he was to be able to deliver that standard, then the preparation of the food had to be of an exceptionally high quality (whilst simultaneously perceived by customers to represent good value for money); customer service and the hotel furnishings and decor – the overall ambience of the whole dining experience had to be just right. And Bill knew that to do all that properly required dedication and concentration.

To this day Bill remains utterly convinced that the most important aspect of running a restaurant is to serve customers what they want to eat. That was why, though some of his celebrity chef colleagues might have thought he was making a grave error of judgement by making a conscious decision to step out of the limelight, he took the view that he needed to focus all his attention on producing the quality of food and the standard of service he felt was required to fill Highgrove.

He did so, having already witnessed countless talented chefs fail to make a success of their own restaurants; a phenomenon he attributes to the fact that some chefs make the mistake of feeding their own egos rather than feeding their customers the kind of dishes they wish to eat, with the inevitable consequence that the popularity of their restaurants soon start to decline.

This contrasts sharply with Bill's customer-centric philosophy of listening to his clientèle and serving them the kind of dishes they request; a philosophy that can only be maintained by the continual adaptation of his offering throughout each of his establishments to match particular trends in the marketplace.

A discernible trend in eating habits over recent years has been a gradual shift towards informality and Bill was quick to adapt to that change. There's a world of difference, though, between adapting to change and slavishly following the latest food fad. Bill is wary of the periodic acclaim awarded to particularly bold and innovative chefs whose recipes may well succeed in firing the imaginations of their peers and food critics but all too often fail to fill restaurants. Food fashion is notoriously fickle and chefs who are quick to jump on the back of any particular bandwagon can soon find themselves facing empty tables.

Bill's view is that the true test of the success of a restaurant is not to gauge its popularity two months after it has opened for business, but to review its performance two years later. A common mistake made by restaurateurs, he suggests, is to invest heavily in their establishments upfront and then sit back for the next few years with the expectation of reaping in the profits with no need for additional outlay.

Bill's philosophy could not be more different. He places a heavy emphasis on continually reinvesting in each of his establishments with a view to improving on the high standards already set. Reinvestment might merely entail the simple things but, as is so often the case, it's the little things that mean a lot: a change of crockery here; a new carpet and curtains there; cleaning the driveway and re-landscaping gardens are of considerable importance when you are catering for a regular clientèle. Perhaps one reason Bill succeeded with Highgrove is that he applied the same principles of managing an efficient kitchen to the management of the hotel. He believes that those chefs with established working disciplines are, in effect, already managers and notes that, during his time at The Caledonian, he had more staff working for him in the kitchen than most hoteliers have working for them in their hotels.

HIGHGROVE HOUSE HOTEL

Bill managed his kitchen at The Caledonian by
departmentalising it. An unapologetic disciplinarian,
kitchen staff knew when to arrive in the morning,
when to go home at night and were quick to learn
what standards were expected of them. Once standards
had been set, the working system ran smoothly.
Whilst he observes that very few kitchens nowadays
are departmentalised, all Bill's are – because it works.
All the chefs at Costley Hotels have worked for the
company over a long period of time. Bill is keen to
encourage his chefs to develop their own particular
styles and will send them to eat out at particular
restaurants to expose them to different cooking
methods and give them fresh ideas.

TOMATO AND BASIL TART

WITH PARMESAN SHAVINGS AND A BALSAMIC DRESSING

(SERVES 4)

Ingredients

4 Shortcrust Pastry
Discs (6cm diameter)

8 Ripe Plum Tomatoes
(thinly sliced)

Mixed Salad Leaves

Balsamic Dressing
(Basic 2.12)

Fresh Parmesan

200g Tapenade
(Basic 2.9)

Pesto (Basic 10)

Red Onion

Spring Onions

Method

- Spread base of pastry discs with tapenade
- Top with layers of thinly sliced plum tomatoes, then sprinkle with pesto
- Slightly warm pastry discs in oven for approx. 8 minutes at 150°C
- Remove from oven
- Arrange on plate with dressed salad leaves, sliced red onions and spring onions
- Top with parmesan shavings and drizzle around balsamic dressing and fresh pesto
- Finish with a few fresh basil leaves

A WARM JERSEY POTATO SALAD

WITH A MEDLEY OF SEAFOOD AND A SAFFRON EMULSION

(SERVES 4)

Ingredients

400g Jersey Potatoes

12 Spring Onions

20g Peas

20g Fresh Coriander

2 Red Peppers

Assorted Fish: 100g
Salmon, 100g Red
Mullet, 100g Wild
Sea Bass, 8 Scallops
and 8 Langoustine

20g Dill

200g Mixed Salad
Leaves (to garnish)

50g Mayonnaise

Fish Veloute (Basic 2.2)

25g Unsalted Butter

50ml Virgin Olive Oil

Sauce

2g Saffron

50ml White Wine

100ml Fish Stock

50g Double Cream

50g Butter

2 Shallots

Salad

- Peel Jersey potatoes and blanch
  (10-12 minutes or until cooked)
- Allow to cool and chop in fine dice
- Mix with spring onions, fresh garden peas,
  chopped coriander and chopped dill
- Bind with a little mayonnaise, fish veloute
  and finely chopped red peppers

Fish

- Delicately cut the fish into bite-sized portions
- Fry in a little virgin oil, finishing with a knob
  of unsalted butter
- Season to taste

Sauce

- Lightly fry the sliced shallots until transparent,
  add white wine and a few sprigs of saffron and
  reduce by two-thirds
- Add fish stock
- Reduce by half
- Add double cream
- Boil for approx. 1-2 minutes, reducing until the sauce
  reaches coating consistency

A Warm Jersey Potato Salad

- Gently add unsalted butter a little bit at a time, whisking the sauce until desired consistency
- Season to taste

To Serve

- Place warm potato salad into a ring mould in centre of plate
- Arrange fish on plate and remove plastic mould
- Drizzle saffron essence around fish
- Finish with a few fresh salad leaves and a sprig of dill

SEARED FILLET OF WILD SEA BASS AND RED MULLET

WITH SURF CLAMS AND ORIENTAL COUSCOUS (SERVES 4)

Ingredients

4 Fillets of Wild Sea Bass

4 Fillets of Red Mullet

8 Surf Clams

200g Couscous

50g Pickled Ginger

2 Fresh Red Chillies

20g Coriander

30ml Sesame Oil

20ml Olive Oil

12 Spring Onions

Red Wine Jus (Basic 2)

50g Sesame Seeds

Fish Stock (Basic 1)

100g Unsalted Butter

Method

- Add the pickled ginger, finely chopped red chillies, chopped spring onions and sesame oil to the couscous
- Season with salt and pepper
- Bring fish stock to the boil, add couscous and mix until light and fluffy
- Add cold knobs of butter and season to taste
- Cover with cling film and leave for 2 minutes
- Lightly pan-fry fish fillets in olive and sesame oil, skin-side down
- Steam surf clams
- Turn the fish fillets (skin side up), sprinkle with sesame seeds and lightly grill
- Warm red wine sauce
- Add the julienne of pickled ginger and chopped coriander

To Serve

- Remove cling film from the couscous and spoon into mould. Invert just off-centre of plate
- Place the fish fillets on top of the couscous
- Arrange surf clams at side
- Pour sauce liberally around the couscous and fish
- Finish with chopped coriander and spring onions

BLANQUETTE OF MUSSELS

WITH FRESH SALMON, PEARL BARLEY RISOTTO

AND A SAFFRON SAUCE (SERVES 4)

Ingredients

300g Fresh Salmon
(skin on - cut into
bite-sized pieces)

1kg Mussels

2 Carrots

2 Courgettes

1 Stick Celery

1kg Pearl Barley

6 Spring Onions

2 Onions

250ml Double Cream

2g Saffron

3 Shallots

50ml Virgin Olive Oil

100ml White Wine

300ml Fish Stock
(Basic 1)

Method

Risotto

- Soak pearl barley for at least 12 hours in cold water
- Finely chop onion, celery, and carrot
- Sweat the vegetables until soft, then add the soaked pearl barley, finely chopped courgettes and sliced spring onions
- De-glaze with white wine and add fish stock gradually
- Keep warm

Mussels

- Wash off excess grit and remove any barnacles from mussels
- Finely slice shallots
- Heat in hot oil taking care not to burn them, and add mussels
- De-glaze with white wine
- Place lid on and cook for 2-3 minutes
- Strain mussels through colander
- Reduce the remaining stock with a little saffron and add double cream

Blanquette of Mussels

- Gently fry the salmon nuggets

- Add mussels and coat with saffron sauce

- Remove from heat and do not re-boil

To Serve

- Place Pearl Barley Risotto in the centre of the plate

- Coat with Blanquette of mussels and salmon

- Add sufficient amount of sauce

- Serve with brown rustic bread (optional)

COCONUT AND LIME CREAM

WITH PINEAPPLE JELLY AND MACADAMIA COOKIE

Ingredients

Cream

100ml Milk

2 Yolks

40g Sugar

Lime Zest and Juice of
1 Lime

100ml Coconut Milk

1.5 leaves or 7.5g
Gelatine

20ml Pineapple Juice

75ml Double Cream

Cookie

125ml Melted Butter

100g Icing Sugar

150g Flour

100g Egg

100g Macadamia Nuts

Sorbet

200ml Coconut milk

300ml Water

200g Sugar

Method

Cream

• Boil milk

• Mix yolks with sugar

• Soak 1 leaf gelatine until soft. Remove from water

• Add milk to yolks

• Add the gelatine to milk and yolks while still hot

• Allow to cool

• Next boil the pineapple juice and soak the remaining half leaf of gelatine. Add to the juice

• Spoon pineapple juice into bottom of moulds (approx 5ml each mould). Allow to set

• Zest and juice the lime, mix with the coconut milk and add to the yolk mixture

• Semi whip cream and fold into the lime and coconut

• Divide between the moulds and chill until set

Cookies

• Chop the nuts quite finely

• Mix flour and icing sugar with the egg

• Fold in the butter and chopped nuts

• Spoon 15g amounts onto kitchen paper (oven-proof) and flatten out approx. 2.5in diameter

• Bake in oven 200°C for 10-12 minutes or until golden

Coconut and Lime Cream

Sorbet

- Boil sugar and water. Allow to cool
- Add the coconut milk and churn in machine
  for 35 minutes
- Freeze

To Serve

- Turn out the coconut cream onto the cookie and
  garnish with pieces of chopped pineapple and
  segments of lime. Can also be served with coconut
  sorbet, zested lime and sticks of caramel sugar

LIGHT POACHED FRUITS

WITH TWO SORBETS (SERVES 4)

Method

- Boil the sugar and water with the lime (approx. 10 minutes)
- Peel and prepare the fruits – pear and pineapple first as they are the hardest and take the longest

  Pear and pineapple into 1 inch chunks

  Kiwi halved

  Mango poached then sliced

  Plums halved

  Mandarin into segments

  Strawberries whole
- Gently poach pineapple and pear for approx. 1 minute
- Remove from heat and add halved kiwi, sliced mango, halved plums and mandarin segments and allow to sit for a further minute
- Divide fruit among the plates
- In the centre place 2 scoops of sorbet, 2 flavours
- Drizzle syrup around

PETIT FOURS

1 ALMOND MACAROONS (MAKES APPROX. 60)

2 ROAST HAZELNUT CLUSTERS (MAKES 10)

3 MARZIPAN LOG (MAKES 50)

Ingredients

300g Ground Almonds

300g Granulated Sugar

3-4 Egg Whites

Method

- Mix almonds with sugar
- Lightly whisk the egg whites and fold into the almonds
- Pipe into $1/4$ inch bulbs onto waxed paper
- Bake until golden in colour at 220°C (approx. 10 mins.)
- Store when cold in airtight container for up to 1 week

Ingredients

40 Whole Hazelnuts
(roasted and peeled)

80g Good Quality Dark
Chocolate

Method

- Gently roast the hazels to a light brown
- Place in a clean tea towel and rub together – the skins will fall off
- Melt the chocolate and mix with the nuts
- Place 4 nuts together in a pyramid onto wax paper and allow to set
- Place in paper cases and store until use

Ingredients

500g White Marzipan

250g Milk Chocolate

100g Icing Sugar

Method

- Divide the marzipan into 5 x 100g blocks
- Roll each one into a sausage – approx. $1/2$ inch wide
- Place onto cling film or wax paper
- Melt the chocolate and brush onto the marzipan
- Allow to set and cut into 1 inch lengths
- Roll in the icing sugar and place into paper cases
- Store until use

CHAPTER THREE

LOCHGREEN COUNTRY HOUSE HOTEL

Once Highgrove House had established itself and was up and running smoothly and profitably, Bill began to scout around for a fresh challenge. One evening, as he was sitting watching television, Bill happened to see a programme about a Walter Mitty-type individual who, amongst other items, had bought himself a mansion house in Troon and an aeroplane, despite the fact that he never had any money. According to the investigative report, the mansion house the individual had 'purchased', shown on-screen, was called Lochgreen House.

The following morning, Bill asked his secretary to find out the exact location of the house. At that time it was virtually impossible to purchase a property in the area and the image Bill had seen on television struck him as an ideal property with which to create a country house hotel of his own, inspired by the Russells' Chapeltoun House in Stewarton.

He duly made contact with the owners of Lochgreen House and drove down from Highgrove to view the property. It soon transpired that he'd driven past the estate on many previous occasions, completely oblivious

to its existence. Bill soon arrived at a verbal agreement
with the owners that, should the Walter Mitty character
featured on the television fail to stump up the promised
cash, then they would sell Lochgreen House to him.

At that time Lochgreen House was a domestic home and
the estate was subdivided into three separate properties,
each privately owned by three different families.

Bill was taking his biggest financial risk to date in
buying Lochgreen House and, once the deal was done,
he had a year-long battle to obtain planning permission
to turn it into a hotel. At the end of that period,
however, the risk and the effort proved to be worthwhile
because he realised that he finally had his dream hotel.
Built in 1905 and set amidst thirty acres of woodland
adjacent to the fairways of Royal Troon Golf Course,
Lochgreen Country House Hotel opened in 1991.

Bill quickly recognised that the purchase of Lochgreen
necessitated the appointment of several key managers
and was soon able to recruit Jim Murdoch as manager of
Lochgreen and Michael Poggi as manager of Highgrove.
Both are now directors of Costley and Costley Hoteliers.
Following graduation from hotel school, Jim Murdoch's

career had started with his appointment as manager of
the Marine Court Hotel in Ayr at the age of twenty-
one. At the age of twenty-five, he was joint owner, in
partnership with his brother-in-law, of Lochinvar Hotel
in Dalry, Kirkcudbrightshire. His career temporarily took
a wrong turning when, in search of a fresh challenge,
he left the catering trade to establish a laundry business.
He was tempted back into the trade he knew best when
Bill offered him the position of manager at Lochgreen.
Michael Poggi's family has always been involved in the
catering trade. The son of an Italian father and a
Scottish mother, his family owns a vineyard in Italy
where they grow tomatoes, and olives to produce olive
oil. Michael had met Bill when they had both worked
at The Hospitality Inn in Irvine, where Michael had
worked in the bar while Bill had worked in the kitchen.
The pair went their separate ways when Michael left
The Hospitality Inn to work elsewhere, before joining
up again when Bill invited him to become involved
with Decanters. Michael then left to open a string of
delicatessens and a new restaurant before being tempted
back to work with Bill as manager of Highgrove, which

remains his base. Bill's next key appointment was to recruit Libby Allison (wife of Jimmy Allison, chef of The Brig o' Doon) as an accountant. Libby and Jimmy's friendship with Bill and his wife dates back to the time when both couples had worked at The Caledonian Hotel in Ayr. On her appointment, Libby took control of the purse strings of the company and established a robust financial accounts department. She is now a director of the company based at Lochgreen, with responsibility for managing the Cochrane Inn.

The first few years at Lochgreen were spent on an extensive refurbishment of the premises, including building completely new kitchens, and on putting the estate back together again. The funds required to carry out this ambitious programme of investment left the company more financially vulnerable than it had ever been before and Bill became concerned at the level of debt involved. However, it was not too long before Lochgreen had been transformed into its present condition and started attracting customers, enabling it to clear its debts and move into profitability. When it opened in 1991, Lochgreen only had seven bedrooms.

This number rose to fifteen in 1995 and there are currently plans afoot for a further twenty-five bedrooms to be incorporated into the spacious estate. A main attraction at Lochgreen is the recently built restaurant which, with its high ceilings and tapestried walls, its chandeliers specially imported from Russia and chairs from Lyon, lends a complementary baronial ambience to the surroundings. Such lavish decor makes Lochgreen a perfect setting for a fine dining experience.

Whilst most country house hotels are located in rural Perthshire or Inverness-shire, Lochgreen is unique in that it blends effortlessly the ambience of a rural retreat with the convenience of having an international airport no more than five minutes' drive away.

Recently awarded three Rosettes and three Red Stars from the AA, Lochgreen House fills a niche for quality at the top end of the market.

SEARED SCALLOPS WITH A BLANQUETTE OF LANGOUSTINES

WITH FINE GREENS AND FRESH PASTA (SERVES 4)

Ingredients

12 Whole Scallops
(shelled and cleaned)

16 Asparagus Tips

8 Langoustine Tails

300g Fresh Samphaire

2 Whole Leeks

1 Bunch of Spring
Onions

400g Fresh Baby
Spinach

300g Fresh Pasta

Fresh Dill

Caviar (optional)

Sauce

100ml White Wine

250ml Fish Stock

150ml Double Cream

3 Shallots

Method

Sauce

- Peel and slice the shallots and sweat them off until transparent. Be careful not to colour them
- Add white wine and reduce by two-thirds
- Add fish stock and again, reduce by half
- Finish with the cream and simmer for 20 minutes
- Pass through fine sieve and season to taste

Dish

- Keep four shells back for presentation of the scallops
- Slice leeks and spring onions into fine rondeles
- Blanch asparagus and samphaire
- Pan fry langoustines
- Add the green vegetables to the pan
- Cover with fish sauce and keep warm. Do not re-boil
- Cook fresh pasta, drain and add a little fish sauce so it coats
- Sear scallops

Seared Scallops with a Blanquette of Langoustines

To Serve

• Arrange pasta, scallops and blanquette of langoustine into the reserved scallop shell and on the plate

• Dress with fresh herbs and a sprig of dill, and finish with caviar if desired

TERRINE OF FOIE GRAS AND DUCK CONFIT

WITH A RED ONION COMPÔTE AND A CELERIAC REMOULADE

Ingredients

300g Fresh Foie Gras

8 Duck Legs

1 Celeriac

6 Red Onions

1 tbsp Redcurrant Jelly

50g Brown Sugar

200ml Red Wine

1 Cinnamon Stick

Mixed Salad Leaves

Truffle Oil (optional)

50g Arran Mustard

50g Mayonnaise

20ml Port

20ml Brandy

Juice of 1 Lemon

Marinade

50ml Red Wine Vinegar

40g Brown Sugar

2 Oranges (halved)

2 Apples (halved)

2 Bay Leaves

4 Sprigs of Thyme

Salt and Pepper

Method

- Duck legs are best prepared two days in advance to maximise flavour

- Place duck legs in roasting tray with all marinade mix, ensuring all the legs are well covered. Cover with cling film and leave for 24 hours

- Cover with vegetable oil and place in pre-heated oven (120°C) for about 15 hours (the longer and slower the legs cook the better)

- Once cooked, remove from the oil, place on a draining rack and cool

- Pick all meat off the bones

- Leave foie gras to come to room temperature

- Using back of knife, de-nerve the foie gras by following the veins down from top to bottom (do not handle too much)

- Place on ovenproof tray, sprinkle with rock salt, pepper and brown sugar

- Drizzle over a little port, brandy and truffle oil and leave to rest for 30-40 minutes

- Place in oven at 200°C for around 6-7 minutes

Terrine of Foie Gras and Duck Confit

- Line terrine mould with cling film, layer with foie gras
  and duck confit to top of terrine, pressing into all the gaps
- Place in fridge and leave to set for at least 12 hours

Red Onion Compôte

- Slice all the red onions very thinly
- Cook off until soft but not coloured then add
  redcurrant jelly, red wine, brown sugar and a
  cinnamon stick and leave to cook over a low
  heat until red wine reduces and leaves a deep
  red syrup texture

Celeriac Remoulade

- Julienne the celeriac into fine strips and season with
  salt and pepper
- Leave for about 10 minutes until it starts to soften
- Mix together mayonnaise and Arran mustard then
  bind all ingredients together with the juice of 1 lemon

To Serve

- Arrange the red onion compôte and celeriac
  remoulade on the plate beside a small bouquet
  of dressed salad leaves
- Place a small slice of the terrine on the plate
  and finish with some truffle oil and some fresh
  ground black pepper

PAN-FRIED FILLET OF SEA TROUT

WITH SMOKED AYRSHIRE BACON AND LEEK RISOTTO

AND A SAFFRON AND CHILLI BUTTER SAUCE

Ingredients

4 Fillets of Sea Trout

Asparagus and Green Beans

Risotto (Basic 4)

11oz Risotto Rice (arborio or carnaloli)

3oz Shallot Purée

2fl.oz Olive Oil (for chicken use truffle oil)

7fl.oz Fish or Chicken Stock

4oz Mascarpone

4oz Finely Grated Parmesan

2fl.oz Double Cream

2 Whole Leeks

6 Rashers of Ayrshire Smoked Bacon (finely sliced)

Sauce (Basic 3)

1 tsp White Wine Vinegar

2 tsp White Wine

2oz Shallot Purée

9oz Cold Unsalted Butter (cubed)

2fl.oz Double Cream

1 Red Chilli

Saffron

Salt and Pepper

Method

- Sear fillets of sea trout
- Blanch asparagus and green beans

Risotto

- Make risotto as recipe and to finish add pan-fried bacon and sautéed leek

Sauce

- Place vinegar, wine, shallot purée in a small pan
- Reduce to a syrup
- Add cream
- Add butter and whisk until amalgamated
- Correct seasoning, strain, then blend with hand blender
- Add finely chopped red chillis and saffron

Pan-Fried Fillet of Sea Trout

To Serve

- Place risotto and sauce on plate

- Finish dish with seared sea trout fillet and fine greens

CASSEROLE OF SEAFOOD

IN A LANGOUSTINE BISQUE WITH SAFFRON POTATOES

AND FRESH BASIL (SERVES 4)

Ingredients

1kg Mussels

8 Scallops

8 Langoustines

4 Grey Mullet
(filleted and scaled)

4 Red Mullet
(filleted and scaled)

100ml White Wine

4 Shallots

4 Cloves of Garlic

Saffron Potatoes

16 Maris Piper Potatoes

50ml Fish Stock

2 Sprigs of Fresh
Saffron

Sauce

Langoustine Bisque
Sauce (Basic 9)

Pesto Sauce (Basic 10)

Method

- Steam the mussels in white wine until open, along with the shallots and garlic
- Remove mussels from liquid and strain liquid into a saucepan
- Cook the fish in the liquid, largest pieces first (grey mullet, red mullet, then langoustine and scallops)
- Once cooked, remove from liquid
- Reduce the stock, add to langoustine bisque and infuse basil in the sauce

To Make Saffron Potatoes

- Peel and turn potatoes into barrel shapes
- Cook in salted water with fish stock and saffron sprigs for 8-10 minutes or until soft

To Serve

- Arrange fish in bowl or plate
- Garnish with fresh asparagus, saffron potatoes and fresh basil leaves
- Add some chilled, unsalted butter, season to taste and drizzle over with pesto sauce

SCOTTISH FILLET OF BEEF

WITH DAUPHINOISE POTATOES AND A GIROLLE

AND MOREL RED WINE JUS (SERVES 4)

Ingredients

4 8oz Fillet Steaks

500g Baby Spinach Leaves

1g Garlic Purée

Salt and Pepper

Nutmeg

Dauphinoise Potatoes (Basic 6)

Red Wine Jus

Basic 2 with the addition of a reduction of red wine, shallots, garlic and thyme finished with blanched girolles and morel mushrooms

Method

- In a hot pan with olive oil, seal fillets of beef top and bottom and on all sides, ensuring good coloration
- For medium rare – place in oven or grill at high temperature for approx. 5-7 minutes
- Cut Dauphinoise potatoes in 4 circles and place in oven to heat approx. 10-15 minutes
- Sauté baby spinach leaves (stalks removed) with a little garlic, salt, pepper and nutmeg

To Serve

- Place Dauphinoise potatoes on a plate to one side
- Add small mound of spinach
- Place medallions of beef on top
- Bring sauce to boil with girolle and morel mushrooms
- Spoon round and drizzle with sauce

HONEY AND SESAME SEED GLAZED BREAST OF DUCK

WITH SAVOY CABBAGE AND A PORT AND BLACKBERRY JUS

Ingredients

4 Breasts of Duck

1 Savoy Cabbage

6 Rashers Smoked Bacon

Garlic

Caraway Seeds

1 Apple (cut and turned)

Sesame Seeds

Honey

12 Cocotte Potatoes

Red Wine Sauce (Basic 2)

Port

Blackcurrants

Thyme

Blackberries

Method

- Slice cabbage into fine strips and remove any hard core
- Very quickly blanche cabbage
- Fry bacon, add cabbage, caraway seeds and garlic
- Pan-fry duck breasts with honey and sesame seeds until skin is crispy and finish in the oven at 180°C until pink
- Very quickly fry the turned apple and blanche cocotte potatoes until golden brown

To Serve

- Place a mound of cabbage off-centre on plate
- Slice duck breast and arrange on plate with apples and potatoes
- Finish with the jus and reduction of port, black-currants, fresh thyme and a few blackberries

costley

CHOCOLATE FONDANT

WITH ORANGE SYRUP (SERVES 4)

Ingredients

20ml Water

15g Glucose Syrup

1 Leaf Gelatine

80g Dark Chocolate

140ml Double Cream

Chocolate Glaze

50ml Boiled Cream

40g Dark Chocolate
(cut into small pieces)

10ml Glucose Syrup

Boil the cream with the
glucose, then pour onto
the chocolate

Once cooled, spoon
over the mousse, and
allow to set

Orange Syrup

100ml Water

200g Sugar

50ml Orange Juice

Boil sugar and water to
a light caramel

Remove from heat and
allow to cool for 2-3
minutes

Carefully add the
orange juice - beware
of spitting

Allow to go cold
before use

Method

- Warm the water with the glucose and soak the gelatine in cold water
- Melt the chocolate in a bowl over warm to hot water (not boiling)
- Semi-whip the cream so it is just beginning to become thick
- Once the water is hot (but not boiling) and the glucose is dissolved, add the soaked gelatine (removed from its own water and drained)
- This liquid is then folded into the melted chocolate and mixed until smooth
- Allow to cool for a few minutes, then fold in whipped cream
- Pour mixture into ring moulds, dariole moulds or even small tea cups (cups should be lined with cling film); chill in fridge or freezer

To Serve

- To garnish the mousse, cover with a 'chocolate glaze' and serve at room temperature with passion fruit sorbet and raspberries

CAPPUCCINO CUP

WITH COFFEE AND BAILEYS MOUSSE (SERVES 4)

Ingredients

20g Flour

26g Icing Sugar

24g Egg White

20g Melted Butter

Method

- Mix flour, icing sugar and egg white together until smooth
- Fold in butter, again mix smooth
- With a piping bag and fine nozzle, pipe mixture into rectangle outline and fill in with a net pattern
- The mix should be piped and baked either on a silicone mat or a well-greased and floured non-stick tray
- Bake at 180°C for 2-3 minutes
- Once golden in colour, carefully remove and mould round a rolling pin to form a ring
- Also, pipe a handle then fix onto cup with chocolate

To serve

- Place biscuit cup onto plate and pipe the mousse inside
- Dust with cocoa powder like a cappuccino
- Garnish plate as desired. I've used field fruits

see page 86 for mousse recipe

COFFEE AND BAILEYS MOUSSE

(SERVES 4)

Ingredients

100ml Double Cream

2 Egg Yolks

30g Sugar

1 Leaf of Gelatine

10ml Baileys

5g Coffee Powder

Method

- Soak gelatine in cold water
- Semi-whip the cream
- Whisk yolks and sugar over a pan of hot water until thick
- Add coffee and Baileys
- Remove from heat and continue to whip until cold
- Remove soaked gelatine
- Fold the cream into egg yolks and then the gelatine
- Allow to set in fridge

To serve

- Place biscuit cup onto plate and using a piping bag with a star nozzle, pipe the mousse inside
- Dust with cocoa powder like a cappuccino
- Garnish plate as desired

SAFFRON POACHED PEAR

WITH REDCURRANTS (SERVES 4)

Ingredients

300ml Water

0.5g Saffron

500g Sugar

0.25g Cinnamon Stick

4 Cornice Pears

Redcurrant Coulis
and Compôte

60g Redcurrants

50g Sugar

10ml Water

Boil all together

Strain out the pulp

Half of the coulis
is for the plates

With the other half,
add another 60g of
redcurrants to make
the compôte

Method

• Boil sugar with water and saffron

• Add cinnamon stick

• Allow the syrup to cool but not to go cold

• Prepare the pears by cutting down either side of the core (approx. 5mm each side of stalk)

• Remove the skin from the core slice. Leave the skin on the two bulb sides

• While the syrup is still warm add the pear pieces, ensuring the skin side of pear is under the syrup

• Cover the pears with a clean cloth or cling film

• Allow syrup and pears to cool to room temperature

The pear is good served with a compôte and coulis of redcurrants with a sorbet and biscuit leaves

To serve

• Take the pears and trim the base of the core so it stands upright. Fan the two bulb sides around the base of the pear. Add the sauce, compôte and sorbet as required. Finish with two leaves of biscuit (for recipe see Cappuccino Cup)

CHAPTER FOUR

THE COCHRANE INN

Throughout his life Bill's twin passions have been catering and football and he has been fortunate in that he has been able to pursue both interests. A life-long supporter of Kilmarnock Football Club, he was honoured when he was invited onto its board (where his accountant Ronnie Hamilton was already a director) by its chairman, Jim Moffat who, with his wife Marjory, was the founder of the travel agency A.T. Mays. When Ronnie resigned from the board in 1997, Bill took over the chair, where he has remained ever since. When Jim Moffat, who had been the mainstay of Kilmarnock Football Club, died, his son Jamie joined the board as a director.

At Gatehead, en- route to a Kilmarnock Football Club board meeting, Bill noticed a derelict pub by a busy roadside. He phoned Libby to find out the asking price and when she returned his call five minutes later with a favourable figure, he put in an offer there and then. So began The Cochrane Inn.

The first thing the company directors did to The Cochrane Inn was to rip it apart and tear it down until only its shell was left standing. Then they completely

rebuilt it from scratch into a small alehouse with a
bar, which has become very popular with passersby
and locals alike.

Bought from receivership for £88,000, Bill spent
£130,000 refurbishing The Cochrane Inn.

An extension which almost doubled the floor capacity
was earmarked for the new kitchen. This was a decision
which very few new owners would have taken – most
would have sought to increase the capacity of the small
restaurant as an obvious means of generating more
revenue – but it was the right decision to take as it
subsequently proved to be the catalyst which enabled
the forty-four seater no-nonsense country pub to serve
up to 250 meals to discerning customers each day.

In fact, the ratio of kitchen floor space to dining area
is far more evenly split throughout all Costley & Costley
Hoteliers' establishments than in most restaurants. Bill
places a great emphasis on devoting space and facilities
to the kitchen brigade and the productivity this has
produced has paid off.

In common with other Costley & Costley
establishments, the chefs at The Cochrane Inn,

Kerr McCallum and John Merrivale, have known Bill over a long period of time. In this case, both were former colleagues at The Caledonian.

With its informal country pub atmosphere, log fire, stone walls and floor, along with the proven recipe of quality food at reasonable prices, The Cochrane Inn opened up a whole new market for Costley & Costley. Designed to be informal and to capture the attention of the hungry passersby, The Cochrane Inn is quite deliberately positioned at a market sector at the opposite end of the spectrum from Lochgreen House.

That said, Costley & Costley's philosophy is that exactly the same management principles and standards of service should apply, whether it is providing good pub fare at good prices or an opulent fine dining experience. The ability to cater for a variety of demands throughout the spectrum of the dining market, all within close proximity of each other, is a critical factor in the success of Costley & Costley Hoteliers.

CHICKEN LIVER PATÉ

FLAVOURED WITH BRANDY AND GOOSE FAT AND SERVED WITH

KUMQUAT PRESERVE (SERVES 10)

Ingredients

2lb Chicken Livers, marinated in Red Wine for 12 hours

8oz Goose Fat

2fl.oz Brandy

1lb Unsalted Butter

3 Cloves of Garlic (crushed)

6 Egg Yolks

1 Pint Double Cream

1oz Ground Coriander

1oz Ground Paprika

1oz Salt and Pepper

Kumquat Preserve

4oz Marmalade

20 Kumquats

2 Shallots (finely chopped)

Dash of Brandy

Combine together in a pot, bring to boil then chill

Method

- Melt butter and goose fat together
- Purée chicken livers, mix with all ingredients and strain through a fine sieve
- Place in lined terrine bowls, cover and place in bain marie in oven for 1hr 40 mins – 2 hrs at 160°C
- Remove and cool
- Cover the top layer of paté with clarified butter and chill, then slice and serve with mixed leaves and a kumquat preserve

costley

GRILLED MACKEREL SALAD

WITH BOILED EGG AND SOURED CREAM (SERVES 4)

Ingredients

4 Medium Mackerel
Fillets

8 Hard Boiled Eggs
(peeled and halved)

1 Romaine Lettuce
(chopped and washed)

Vinaigrette Dressing
(Basic 2.10)

4oz Soured Cream

Pesto (Basic 10)

Balsamic Dressing
(Basic 2.12)

2 Carrots (sliced and
blanched)

Chives

Method
- Slice mackerel and place under hot grill for 2-3 minutes each side

To Serve
- Mix Romaine lettuce with vinaigrette dressing
- Place in centre of plate. Arrange mackerel fillets on salad, garnish with boiled eggs and carrots
- Combine pesto with soured cream and dot around plate for garnish. Finish with chopped chives and balsamic dressing

ROAST CHICKEN

WITH POMME PURÉE, BACON LARDONS

AND CARAMELISED SHALLOTS (SERVES 4)

Ingredients

4 8oz Chicken
Supremes

Pomme Purée
(Basic 5)

8oz Shallots

4 Bacon Strips

12 Roast Potatoes

Red Wine Sauce
(Basic 2)

Sprigs of Thyme

Method
- Trim chicken, pan fry on both sides and place in hot oven for 8-10 minutes
- Caramelise shallots with butter and brown sugar and place in oven along with the chicken
- Fry bacon

To Serve
- Pipe pomme purée on to plate
- Slice chicken
- Garnish with caramelised shallots, bacon and roast potatoes and fresh sprigs of thyme
- Drizzle with red wine sauce

costley

SAUERKRAUT AND FRANKFURT SAUSAGE

(SERVES 2)

Ingredients

1 Jar of Sauerkraut

2 Large Frankfurt Sausages

10 New Ayrshire Potatoes

Red Wine Sauce

8oz Button Mushrooms

Fresh Chives

Garlic

Olive Oil

Method

- Cook new potatoes in salted water
- Grill Frankfurt sausage
- Warm Sauerkraut
- Sauté mushrooms in a little garlic and olive oil

Serve

- Place Sauerkraut in centre of plate
- Slice sausage and arrange on top
- Serve with new potatoes
- Add mushrooms, red wine sauce and garnish with chopped chives

BREAD PUDDING

(SERVES 10)

Ingredients

500ml Milk

500ml Double Cream

6 Egg Yolks

4 Eggs

200g Sugar

1 Vanilla Pod
(split and seeded)

100g Sultanas

250g Brioche Bread

Method

- Mix egg yolks, whole eggs, sugar and vanilla seeds
- Gently warm the cream and milk together
- Pour onto the egg mix and combine gently – don't whisk
- In an oven-proof dish sprinkle 100g of sultanas
- Cut and lay the brioche bread in the dish in a single overlapping layer
- Strain over the filling and allow to soak for 10 minutes. Top up and cook in a bain marie for 30 minutes at 170°C
- To finish, either glaze with apricot jam, castor sugar or icing sugar. I prefer the latter

To serve

- In a warm bowl place some fresh custard, then onto this set a piece of the pudding and dust with icing sugar
- To finish, place a scoop of vanilla or honey ice cream on top

STICKY TOFFEE PUDDING

(SERVES 6)

Ingredients

3lb Dates

1 Pint Water

1 Block Unsalted Butter

18oz Sugar

2lb Self Raising Flour

4-5 tsp Baking Soda

6 Eggs

Toffee Sauce

200ml Water

200g Sugar

300ml Cream

Boil sugar and water to a dark caramel.

Carefully stir in the cream (beware of liquid rising up the pan).

Warm before use

Method

- Boil the dates in water
- Cream sugar and butter together
- Add flour and combine
- Add the baking soda to the dates then add the eggs
- Mix everything together
- Cook at Gas mark 4 for 1 hour

To Serve

- Warm pudding and place on warm plate
- Pour toffee sauce over
- Garnish with vanilla ice cream and mint

CHAPTER FIVE

THE BRIG O' DOON

It was around the time of the reconstruction of The Cochrane Inn that The Burns Monument Hotel in Alloway was put up for sale. Despite its location in the heart of Burns' country, the hotel was being run by Macdonald Hotels on a management contract basis and had been underperforming for a number of years. Before submitting a bid for the hotel, Bill went on holiday, where he subsequently fell ill, forcing him to postpone his plans for expansion. In the interim, The Burns Monument Hotel was purchased by a new owner. However, when Bill had fully recovered a few months later, he bought the hotel from its new owner and renamed it The Brig o' Doon.

He now had two developments on the go at the same time – The Cochrane Inn and The Brig o' Doon – not an ideal situation to be in because it stretched the company's resources to the limit and divided the effort which could be devoted to each project. But at least Highgrove and Lochgreen were within a few miles of the two new projects, making it possible to supervise what was going on.

As with all his previous projects, Bill decided to invest heavily in renovating The Brig o' Doon, which had fallen into a state of disrepair. In so doing, he was simply continuing a long history of renovation and alteration to the building.

Erected in 1829, the building was originally named The Burns Arms Inn. Records show that, in 1837, a sculptured head (now placed above the pre-dinner drinks bar), which may have been by the local self-taught artist James Thom (responsible for the statues of Tam o' Shanter and Souter Johnnie which are resident in the hexagonal building in the Burns Monument gardens) was placed in the gardens.

The original building was altered in 1903-4 to designs prepared by the architect Allan Stevenson and was further extended in 1924 to provide for the addition of seven bedrooms. In 1947 a small extension to the south gave independent access to the bar from Alloway, with more extensive alterations undertaken in 1953 to the designs of John Murray, architect in Troon, in the form of a large tea room, lounge bar, plus bar with new kitchen, entrance hall and vestibule accessible from

Millbrae. This formed the inherited accommodation purchased by Bill in November 1996.

In January 1997 the hotel was demolished with the exception of the front facade which has a C listing. Bill credits the sympathetic scheme designed by the Ayr-based architectural practice, the Alastair Murdoch Partnership, as a huge contributory factor to the success of the hotel.

The Brig o' Doon now has a restaurant with seating for a hundred diners, a function suite with seating for two hundred, a coffee shop seating forty and five bedrooms. Its location and baronial banqueting hall with its views of the River Doon and the Brig o' Doon – the setting for the conclusion to Robert Burns' famous tale, 'Tam o' Shanter' – has ensured the hotel's popularity as a wedding venue. Indeed, it played host to some 170 weddings in 1999, a figure which looks set to be maintained.

The Brig o' Doon was deliberately bought with the intention of transforming it into a venue catering for large functions; a market niche that Costley & Costley had yet to address. It was Jim Murdoch who first spotted the obvious potential of the unique location as a sought after venue for wedding parties.

The new Brig o' Doon House Hotel opened its doors to the public in late September 1997. In 1999, the Banks o' Doon coffee shop, flower shop and gift shop opened overlooking the gardens and river. There are plans to put a bandstand in the garden and serve afternoon tea, a popular means of whiling away a few hours in the open air on that very site in an earlier incarnation.

The two chefs at Brig o' Doon are Jimmy Allison, who has a long association with Bill, and Ian Ferguson, formerly the head chef at Lochgreen.

Bill describes Brig o' Doon as the biggest and best investment he's ever made. Despite only having five bedrooms, a number which would have dissuaded many hoteliers from expressing an interest, the Brig o' Doon is the most profitable of all the Costley & Costley establishments and, as such, stands as a fitting testament to the company's opportunist purchasing strategy.

SCALLOP, TOMATO AND FETA SALAD

(SERVES 4)

Ingredients

8 Plum Tomatoes

Basil Leaves

100g Baby Asparagus

200g Feta Cheese

1 dozen Scallops

250g Mixed Salad Leaves

Balsamic Dressing (Basic 2.12)

Olive Oil

8oz Freshly Grated Parmesan

Method

- Sear scallops
- Slice tomatoes
- Blanch asparagus and refresh in cold water (approx. 8 minutes)
- Form parmesan into a circle on a silicone mat and bake in 180°C oven for 5-6 minutes until golden brown
- Remove from mat and allow to cool

To Serve

- Combine tomato, mixed leaves, seared scallops, feta cheese, asparagus and basil leaves and drizzle with balsamic dressing and olive oil
- Season with salt and pepper

LIGHTLY CURRIED COD FILLET

WITH CORIANDER RISOTTO AND A LEMON GRASS BUTTER SAUCE

(SERVES 4)

Ingredients

Risotto

400g Arborio Rice

100ml White Wine

400ml Fish Stock

2 Shallots
(finely chopped)

50g Mascarpone Cheese

8 Coriander Seeds
(crushed)

20g Fresh Coriander

50g Unsalted Butter

40g Freshly Grated
Parmesan

Fish

4 x 200-220g Cod Fillet

50g Mild Madras Curry
Powder

10ml Virgin Olive Oil

Sauce

50g Shallots
(finely chopped)

2 Cloves of Garlic
(finely chopped)

50ml White Wine
Vinegar

100ml Dry White Wine

50ml Cold Water

200g Unsalted Butter
(chilled and diced)

2 Sticks of Lemon
Grass (roughly diced)

Juice of ½ a Lemon

Salt and Pepper

Method

• Do not wash the rice

• Sweat the chopped shallots and crushed coriander
  seeds in a little butter for approx 1 minute with
  no coloration

• Add rice and stir for further minute ensuring
  no coloration

• Add white wine and reduce by two-thirds

• On a medium heat add a ladle at a time of warmed
  fish stock until the rice is cooked (10-15 minutes)

• Once rice has reached a soft texture with a slight bite,
  add the mascarpone cheese, fresh coriander and grated
  parmesan. The risotto should be of a creamy texture
  but not too wet

• In a small heavy-bottomed saucepan combine shallots,
  garlic, white wine vinegar, lemon grass and white
  wine and boil until there is approx 1 tablespoon of
  liquid left

• Add the cold water (this will help the emulsion)

• Over a gentle heat whisk in the cold diced butter, a
  little at a time, until completely amalgamated

• The finished sauce will be creamy and homogenous
  and a delicate lemon yellow colour

Lightly Curried Cod Fillet

- Season with a tiny amount of salt, pepper and a squeeze of lemon juice
- Pass through a fine sieve and keep warm

To Serve

- In a hot frying pan add olive oil. Season the cod fillets with salt, pepper and mild Madras curry powder and sear the cod fillets, skin-side down first – allow 4-5 minutes – turn the fish and place in the oven for a further 5 minutes at 200°C
- In the centre of a plate place the risotto rice. On top, place cod fillet and drizzle with butter sauce. Garnish with fresh peas, asparagus and spring onions

CONFIT OF DUCK WITH HORSERADISH POTATO PURÉE

SERVED WITH A PEARL BARLEY BROTH JUS (SERVES 4)

Ingredients

4 Duck Legs (knuckle removed and bone cleaned)

600g Maris Piper Potatoes

50g Fresh Horseradish

100g Pearl Barley

100g Carrots (finely diced)

100g Leek (finely diced)

500ml Red Wine Jus (Basic 2)

100g Unsalted Butter

50ml Double Cream

1ltr Goose Fat or Vegetable Oil

Marinade

150ml Red Wine Vinegar

1 Bulb of Garlic (cut in half)

6 Bay Leaves

8 Star Anise

30g Coriander Seeds

50g Demerara Sugar

1 Carrot (roughly chopped)

1 Onion (roughly chopped)

Method

• Place duck legs and all the marinade mix in a container, mix well and leave for 24 hours

• Put the duck legs and marinade into a small roasting tin and cover with the goose fat or vegetable oil and place into a pre-heated oven at 120°C for about 12-14 hours

• Peel and boil the potatoes in salted water, drain and pass the potatoes through a drum sieve

• Soak the barley for around 4-6 hours in cold water. Drain, wash and cook in salted water for about 30-40 minutes

• Gently fry the finely chopped leek and carrots in a little oil and add the cooked barley

• Put potato purée back into a small pan, add the double cream and unsalted butter with the finely grated fresh horseradish

• Season to taste

Confit of Duck with Horseradish Potato Purée

To Serve

- Remove duck legs from the oil and place on a cloth to remove excess oil
- Spoon potato purée on to the plate and place confit duck leg next to it
- Heat red wine jus and add pearl barley mix and drizzle onto the plate
- Garnish with blanched green beans and turned carrots for colour

BANANA AND CINNAMON PUDDING WITH CARAMEL SAUCE

(SERVES 4)

Ingredients

110g Butter

110g Sugar

2 Eggs

1 Large Banana (puréed)

125g Self Raising Flour

10g Cinnamon Powder

Caramel Sauce

300ml Water

200g Sugar

150ml Double Cream

Juice of ½ a Lemon

Method

- Cream the butter and sugar together until fluffy
- Add eggs slowly and beat smooth
- Sieve the flour and cinnamon and add to the butter mix
- Add the banana purée, mix until smooth
- Divide mixture between buttered and floured individual pudding moulds
- Cover in foil and place in a pot with water halfway up the mould, cover with the lid and steam for 20-25 minutes

Caramel Sauce

- Boil sugar and water to a dark caramel
- Brush sides of pan with lemon juice – to stop crystallisation
- Remove from heat and allow to cool for 2 minutes
- Carefully whisk in the cream

To Serve

- Turn out puddings from mould onto warmed bowls
- Cover with caramel sauce, top with sugar, glazed banana slices and vanilla ice cream

LEMON TART

WITH KUMQUAT COMPÔTE

(SERVES 8-10)

Ingredients	Compôte
8 Large Eggs	300g Kumquats
3 Lemons (juice)	100ml Water
600ml Double Cream	200g Sugar
170g Sugar	1 Vanilla Pod
Sweet Paste Tart Sheet (10 inch part-baked)	
Castor Sugar (for dusting)	

Method

• Mix all ingredients together and strain

• Pour mix into tart shell and bake gently for
  20 minutes at 170°C

• Allow to cool at room temperature

Compôte Method

• Wash and halve the kumquats

• Remove seeds

• Add the kumquats to the sugar, water and vanilla pod
  and bring to boil

• Allow to boil for 2-3 minutes

• Remove any scum and reduce – simmer for approx.
  45-60 minutes

• Allow to reduce and thicken but not caramelise

• Remove from heat and cool. If too thick add water

To serve

• Dust tart with castor sugar and glaze under a very hot
  grill (or use a blowlamp). Cut the tart and serve on
  plate, adding a spoonful of compôte and either fresh
  whipped cream or a lemon sorbet

BASIC RECIPES 1

BASIC 1
FISH STOCK (MAKES 4 PINTS)

4lb Flat Fish Bones

White of Small Leek (finely chopped)

1 Large Celery Stalk (finely chopped)

1 Onion (finely chopped)

1 Fennel Bulb (sliced)

1 tbs Olive Oil

1/2 pint White Wine

Enough water to cover

1 Lemon (sliced)

Parsley Stalks

- Wash and chop bones
- Sweat off veg, parsley stalks and lemon in oil
- Add bones, wine then water
- Simmer and skim for 20 minutes
- Leave to infuse then strain

BASIC 2
RED WINE SAUCE (MAKES 4 PINTS)

1 Bottle of Red Wine

8oz Meat Trimmings

4 Onions (sliced)

1 Carrot

1 Celery

Olive Oil

2 Sprigs of Thyme

2 Bay Leaves

1 Garlic Bulb (halved)

2 litres Brown Stock

4oz Sugar

Double Cream

- In large pan brown off the trimmings and mirepoix (finely chopped onion, carrot and celery) in a little olive oil until they start to caramelise
- De-glaze using a little red wine at a time (this will keep the caramelisation and add colour to the sauce)
- Once the wine sauce is reduced (until almost dry) add the sugar, herbs, garlic and stock, then reduce by half
- Strain through muslin into a clean pot
- Reduce again to correct consistency
- Adjust seasoning and add few drops of double cream to give depth and shine

BASIC 3

BEURRE BLANC (MAKES 1/2 PINT - SERVES 4)

1 tsp White Wine Vinegar

2 tsp White Wine

2oz Shallot Purée

2fl.oz Double Cream

9oz Cold Unsalted Butter (cubed)

Salt and Pepper

- Place vinegar, wine, shallot purée in a small pan
- Reduce to a syrup
- Add cream
- Add butter and whisk until amalgamated
- Correct seasoning, strain, then blend with hand-blender

BASIC 4

RISOTTO (SERVES 4-6)

11oz Risotto Rice (arborio or carnaloli)

3oz Shallot Purée

2fl.oz Olive Oil (for chicken use truffle oil)

7fl.oz Fish Stock or Chicken Stock

4oz Mascarpone

4oz Finely Grated Parmesan

2fl.oz Double Cream

3fl.oz White Wine

- Sweat off shallot and rice with the oil
- Add white wine and reduce. Add desired stock and reduce slowly until rice is cooked (7-8 minutes)
- Add double cream (this will cool the risotto and stop the cooking)
- Off the heat, fold in mascarpone and parmesan

BASIC 5
POMME PURÉE (SERVES 6)

8 Large Potatoes

Salt and Pepper

6oz Butter

2oz Double Cream

- Simmer potatoes until tender
- Drain off potatoes
- Pass through sieve
- Adjust seasoning and beat in 4oz butter
- When ready to use, heat in a small pan
  then beat in remaining cream and butter

BASIC 6
DAUPHINOISE POTATOES (SERVES 8)

4lb Potatoes (peeled
and sliced thinly)

1 pint Milk

8fl.oz Double Cream

Finely Grated Parmesan

Salt and Pepper

Butter

- Line a large roasting tray with soft butter
- Layer with potatoes, season and sprinkle with cheese
- Continue layering and seasoning until potatoes are finished
- Bring milk and cream to the boil until the mixture thickens
- Cover potatoes with cream
- Cover top layer with more parmesan
- Place into oven at 180°C for 45 minutes

For Lemon Dauphinoise –
sprinkle each layer with lemon zest
For Garlic Dauphinoise –
sprinkle each layer with garlic purée

BASIC 7

CHICKEN STOCK (MAKES 4 PINTS)

Chicken Carcasses (roasted in oven for brown stock or left as they are for white stock)

6 Pigs' Feet

Carrot, Onion, Celery and Leek (roughly chopped)

Bulb of Garlic (halved)

White Peppercorns, Bay Leaf, Coriander Seeds, Mustard Seeds

Bouquet Garni (1 sprig of thyme, 1 sprig of rosemary, 4 parsley stalks, 1 sprig of tarragon tied with string)

- Place all ingredients into a stock pot, cover with cold water and bring to boil. Simmer for 6 hours skimming as necessary

BASIC 8

BEEF/VEAL STOCK (MAKES 4 PINTS)

Beef or Veal bones, browned

Carrot, Onion, Celery and Leek (roughly chopped and roasted until caramelised)

6 Chopped Plum Tomatoes

Bulb of garlic (halved)

White Peppercorns, Bay Leaf, Coriander Seeds, Mustard Seeds

Bouquet Garni (1 sprig of thyme, 1 sprig of rosemary, 4 parsley stalks, 1 sprig of tarragon tied with string)

- Place all ingredients into a stock pot, cover with cold water and bring to boil
- Simmer for 6-8 hours skimming as necessary
- Pork, Lamb and Game Stocks are same recipe and method as above
- Game stock – add juniper berries

BASIC 9
LANGOUSTINE BISQUE (MAKES 4 PINTS)

60g Butter

30g Shallots
(very finely sliced)

30g Button Mushrooms

8 Crayfish or
Langoustine Heads,
Raw or Cooked (finely
chopped)

1 tbsp Cognac

75ml Dry White Wine

150ml Fish Stock

Small Bouquet Garni
and Sprig of Tarragon

40g Ripe Tomatoes
(peeled and deseeded)

Pinch of Cayenne
Pepper

150ml Double Cream

Salt and Freshly
Ground Pepper

- In a shallow saucepan melt 20g butter over a low heat
- Add chopped shallots and mushrooms
  and sweat for 1 minute
- Add crayfish or langoustine heads to pan, increase
  heat and fry briskly for 2-3 minutes stirring
  continuously with a spatula
- Pour in Cognac, ignite with a match, add the wine
  and reduce by half, then pour in fish stock
- Bring to boil, then lower heat so that sauce bubbles
  gently. Add bouquet garni, tomato, cayenne and
  smidgeon of salt and cook for 30 minutes
- Stir in cream and bubble sauce for another 10 minutes
- Remove bouquet garni, transfer contents of pan to
  a food processor for 2 minutes. Strain sauce through
  fish-mesh conical sieve into clean saucepan, rubbing
  it through with back of ladle
- Bring sauce back to boil and season with salt
  and pepper
- Off heat, whisk in remaining butter, a little at a time
  until sauce is smooth and glossy
- It is now ready to serve

BASIC 10

PESTO SAUCE (MAKES 120ML)

3 Garlic Cloves (peeled
and halved with green
shoots removed)

15 Basil Leaves

75g Freshly Grated
Parmesan

110ml Olive Oil

Salt and Freshly
Ground Pepper

- In a small mortar, crush garlic to a purée with a pinch of salt (or use blender)
- Add basil and crush or blend to a homogeneous paste
- Add parmesan
- Trickle the olive oil in a steady stream, stirring continuously with the pestle as though making mayonnaise
- Work sauce until smooth
- Season to taste with salt and pepper

Use pesto immediately or transfer to a bowl and cover with cling film. It will keep in the fridge for several days

CHAPTER SEVEN

BASIC RECIPES 2

BASIC 2.1

COURT BOUILLON (MAKES 1 PINT)

3 Leeks (coarsely chopped)

8 White Peppercorns

1 Carrot

Parsley Stalks

1 Stick of Celery

$\frac{1}{4}$oz Salt

3 Onions

Zest of 1 Lemon

2 Fennel Bulbs

1 Star Anise

Sprig of Thyme

2fl.oz White Wine

- Place all vegetables and herbs in a large pan, cover with water and bring to boil
- Add lemon zest, anise, white wine and salt
- Simmer for 35 minutes then strain and store

BASIC 2.2

FISH VELOUTE (MAKES 2 PINTS)

2 pints Fish Stock

4oz Shallot Purée

1 pint White Wine

1$\frac{1}{2}$ pints Double Cream

1 pint Noily Prat

Juice of $\frac{1}{2}$ Lemon

1oz Unsalted Butter

- Sweat off shallots with the butter
- Reduce white wine by two-thirds
- Add Noily Prat and reduce by a further two-thirds
- Add fish stock and reduce by half
- Add double cream and the juice of $\frac{1}{2}$ a lemon

BASIC 2.3

CHICKEN SAUCE (MAKES 3 PINTS)

2 pints Chicken Stock

Juice of ½ a Lemon

4oz Shallot Purée

1 pint Double Cream

2 Sprigs of Fresh Thyme

1 pint Dry Sherry

2oz Cold Butter

1 pint White Wine

- Sweat off shallots with the thyme
- Reduce the wine and sherry by two-thirds
- Add chicken stock. Reduce by half
- Add cream and lemon juice
- Bring to the boil, strain and whisk in butter

BASIC 2.4

TOMATO COULIS (MAKES 1 PINT)

7oz Plum Tomatoes

Dash of Tabasco

2fl.oz Red Wine Vinegar

Dash of Tomato Ketchup

1oz Tomato Purée

2fl.oz Olive Oil

- Blend all ingredients to a purée
- Add oil and blend for 30 seconds
- Pass three times through fine strainer until smooth

BASIC 2.5

TOMATO FONDUE (MAKES 1/2 LITRE)

8 Large Ripe Plum
Tomatoes

1 Garlic Clove
(crushed)

3fl.oz Olive Oil

1 Sprig of Thyme

1 Shallot (finely
chopped)

- Blanche plum tomatoes for 10 seconds in boiling water
- Remove skin
- Cut tomatoes into quarters and deseed
- Chop remaining flesh into small dice
- Sweat the garlic and shallot in the oil
- Add chopped tomatoes and thyme
- Cook gently, until moisture has been reduced

BASIC 2.6

HOLLANDAISE SAUCE (MAKES 1/2 PINT) SERVES 4

4 Whole Eggs

2 Blocks of Butter
(clarified)

1 tbsp White Wine
Vinegar

Salt and Pepper

- In a round-based bowl over a pan of hot water, whisk eggs, vinegar, salt and pepper until doubled in volume and reached ribbon stage
- Slowly add clarified butter and season to taste

BASIC 2.7

MAYONNAISE (MAKES 750ML)

1 tbsp Dijon Mustard

1 pint Olive Oil

2 tbsp White Wine
Vinegar

1 pint Vegetable Oil

4 Whole Eggs

- In a food processor, blend eggs, mustard and vinegar
- Slowly add the oil until it becomes thick
- Remove then store

BASIC 2.8

SAUCE VIERGE (MAKES 120ML)

3fl.oz Basil Oil

8 Basil Leaves Julienne

1fl.oz Lemon Juice

2 Tomatoes (concasse)

1 tsp Crushed
Coriander Seeds

- Follow stages 1-3 of recipe 2.5 above
- Heat the oil gently then add lemon juice
- Remove from heat
- Add coriander seeds and leave to infuse in the oil
- Add basil leaves and tomato concasse then serve

BASIC 2.9
TAPENADE (SERVES 4)

9oz Good Black Olives

1 Garlic Clove

2oz Anchovies

2 tsp Olive Oil

1oz Capers

- Place all ingredients apart from oil into a blender until smooth
- Add oil then store as for pesto

BASIC 2.10
VINAIGRETTE (SERVES 4)

1 tsp Dijon Mustard

2fl.oz Water

4fl.oz Walnut Oil

2fl.oz Wine Vinegar

4fl.oz Olive Oil

- Whisk together all ingredients to form an emulsion

BASIC 2.11

TRUFFLE VINAIGRETTE (SERVES 4)

4fl.oz Truffle Oil

Salt and Pepper

1fl.oz Tarragon Vinegar

1 tsp Truffata (optional)

4fl.oz Water

- Whisk together all ingredients to form an emulsion

BASIC 2.12

BALSAMIC DRESSING

6fl.oz Balsamic Vinegar

Salt and Pepper

15fl.oz Virgin Olive Oil

- Reduce balsamic vinegar by two-thirds
- Leave to cool
- Whisk in olive oil and season to taste

CHAPTER EIGHT

THE ENTREPRENEUR

The Cochrane Inn and The Brig o' Doon both opened
in 1997 and, once they were up and running, Bill
decided to increase his investment in Kilmarnock
Football Club. He is now building a new fifty-bedroom
hotel in Kilmarnock (his first involvement in a new
building, but not necessarily his last), with banqueting
for five hundred and a new fitness centre. He has also
added an equestrian centre at Symington to his stable
of investments, which he intends to turn into a football
academy for the youth side of the club.

Kilmarnock Football Club is the one area in which
Bill has invested where he is not anticipating a return,
but he is seeking to develop and diversify the
infrastructure of the club to enable the attraction
of alternative streams of revenue. He approaches the
running of the football club as a business, and is acutely
aware that its success is dependent upon the quality
of the performance of its players on the park on any
given Saturday afternoon. No matter how efficiently
and prudently he can organise the off-pitch activities
of the club, it is the on-pitch performance, over
which he exercises no control, which will ultimately
determine its fate.

Bill did not invest in Kilmarnock Football Club to make money. Rather, he sees it as a way of contributing something back to the local economy and community which has been good for his business. His aim is to apply the same philosophy upon which he has built Costley & Costley Hoteliers – a comprehensive application of high housekeeping standards combined with a zealous attention to detail – to Kilmarnock Football Club.

He suggests that walking into a football stadium should feel like walking into a hotel since both belong to the same leisure business and, as such, every day brings with it fresh challenges and its own need for excellence. Just as Kilmarnock Football Club cannot allow complacency to creep in after a string of good results on the park, neither can any of Costley & Costley's establishments afford to rest on their laurels and bask in the glow of past achievements.

Bill places great emphasis on the fact that, if any given guest arrives for lunch on any given day, then he has the right to expect to receive a consistently high standard of service, irrespective of whether his chosen restaurant has

been particularly busy the day before or is in the midst of preparations for a large function that same evening. Whilst such instances might well pose real challenges for staff, neither are of any concern to the guest in question, who should remain oblivious to any extraordinary circumstances taking place behind the scenes. Complacency cannot afford to be allowed to creep in under any circumstances because it would then threaten the premise on which the whole business is built.

It is Costley & Costley Hoteliers' drive for high standards through immaculate housekeeping and attention to detail – from the strategic placing and arrangement of fresh flowers to the manicured lawns and the well-stocked log fires – that unifies each of its four establishments, whichever market sector each is designed to serve.

Despite this pervasive, unifying characteristic, each of the firm's establishments has its own deliberately distinct character, ranging from the traditional Scottish pub type ambience of The Cochrane Inn providing good food at sensible prices at one end of the spectrum, all the way through to the exclusive, luxurious fine dining experience offered by Lochgreen Country House Hotel at the other.

The distinctiveness of each of his establishments is considered by Bill to be a critical factor in the ongoing success of the company. He feels that there would be little point of further expansion if investment in new premises served only to displace custom from his existing portfolio. It is in order to avoid precisely this scenario that it is considered an absolute necessity for each of Bill's establishments to find their own particular market niche. Given the close geographical proximity of his various business interests, avoiding overlap is much easier said than done, but it is a skill that Costley & Costley has developed to great effect over the years and goes a long way towards explaining the wisdom of Bill's opportunist purchasing policy.

All the establishments are located within an eighteen-mile radius in Ayrshire. Such close proximity of his businesses enables Bill to visit each of them every day. He is very much a hands-on proprietor and will often cook in one of his kitchens.

Costley & Costley has grown rapidly over recent years, but there is no sign of this growth rate diminishing. Rather, Bill's view is that the company now has the infrastructure necessary to facilitate future expansion. Indeed, as this book was going to press, he announced the purchase of a public house in Troon called The Burns Tavern and, in partnership with Brian Sage (the owner of Wilding's restaurant in Girvan) the 120-seat Balkenna Fish Restaurant at Turnberry, overlooking Arran.

The growth of Costley & Costley Hoteliers to date has, to a large extent, been driven by Bill's insatiable desire for progress and quest for new challenges to conquer and there is no reason to suggest that this desire will ever be satiated.

Bill's ambition for growth, and that of his family and the other directors of the company, remains strong. It may well have a payroll approaching three hundred full-time employees, yet Costley & Costley remains very much a family business. All the directors of the company have known each other for so long now that a familial sensibility of team work and communal effort has infiltrated the workplace. Bill is proud of Costley &

Costley and his hope is that everyone involved in it is proud of it too. Guests tend to agree that such pride is justified. Indeed, the familial sensibility extends to guests too, with Bill making the point that, over any given weekend, Costley & Costley will serve up to two thousand meals to a loyal clientèle drawn, for the most part, from the local community in Ayrshire who feel very much part of the company and most of whom are known to his front-of-house staff by name. Ultimately, though, the secret of Costley & Costley's success can be summed up in four little words, the words of its motto: the pursuit of excellence. It is this pursuit that has led Bill Costley to realise that rarely achieved transition: from a par excellence chef to an exceptional entrepreneur.

LIST OF RECIPES